Basic Transformation

A Small Group Bible
Study on the Basics of
Christianity and
Transformation

By Mark Ballenger

Welcome

By transformation, I simply mean "change." How does real life-change occur?

God changes us in a moment when we put our faith in Jesus and we become a new creation, "This means that anyone who belongs to Christ has become a new person. The old life is gone; a new life has begun!" (2 Corinthians 5:17).

In another sense, God continues to change us throughout our lifetime, "So all of us who have had that veil removed can see and reflect the glory of the Lord. And the Lord— who is the Spirit—makes us more and more like him as we are changed into his glorious image" (2 Corinthians 3:18).

In this small group Bible study, we will look at the fundamentals of the Christian faith while paying special attention to how these basic truths affect our transformation.

This small group Bible study is divided into 8 weeks. Each week is divided into three sections: the what, the why, and the how. Each of these sections have two discussion questions. At the end of each chapter are four additional reflection questions. I suggest each person studies the chapter individually throughout the week, perhaps breaking up each chapter over three days. Then as a group you can have discussions stemming from the ten questions which each group member completed on their own. But feel free to do what works for you. The study was designed to be flexible.

My goal was to create a study in simple language that anyone could benefit from. I also wanted to make it as concise as possible. Therefore more could have been said, but I believe the "basics" for transformation are present.

He alone can transform us, and oh how desperately we need him.

For his glory and our good,
Mark

Table of Contents

Week 1
The Transforming Power of the Gospel
Key Text: Ephesians 2:1-10

Getting Started: In your opinion, why are there so many problems in the world? What's the main problem?

What Is the Gospel?

Why are there so many problems in this world? Every religion, scientist, philosopher, and politician has tried to answer this question and offer solutions. While there are massive disagreements about what is the real problem on this planet, there is little disagreement that there is a big problem. We all know things are not the way they are supposed to be, both in the whole universe and in our own lives.

People know they are not supposed to break the law, and yet they do. We know we should not be mean to the people we love, and yet we are. We may know we are not supposed to be addicted to anything, but the addiction remains despite our best efforts. We know there shouldn't be hungry people on the streets with nowhere to live, but despite societies continued hard word, there always has been a problem of homelessness.

The Bible gives us a clear answer about humanity's problem and a clear solution that has transformed the lives of millions of people. God is on the move. He desires to save people. He loves you. He wants to help you through this world. And most of all he wants to transform you for his glory.

But before we can truly appreciate his solution found in Jesus Christ, the one solution that can change everything, we first need to understand the real problem we face on this planet. In one word, the primary problem every human faces on this planet is "sin."

Everything is messed up in this world because of human sin. From individual problems to problems we as a whole society face, it all eventually comes back to the problem of sin. Sin has corrupted everything and made this world very different than the way God first made it and wanted it to be. So what is human sin, when did it start, and what problems has it caused?

Sin is a word that can be defined in many ways, but at its core, sin is not loving God. This lack of love is also known as disobeying God (John 14:23-24). Sin causes our relationship with God to be broken.

In the beginning, God created Adam and Eve to be in an intimate relationship with himself and to rule over creation as they reflected his image. God loved humans from the start, and because he loved them he gave them commands that were for their protection and that would benefit their relationship with him. In Genesis 2:16-17 it reads:

> *But the Lord God warned him, "You may freely eat the fruit of every tree in the garden—[17] except the tree of the knowledge of good and evil. If you eat its fruit, you are sure to die."*

Sadly, Adam and Eve did not listen to God, they did not love him, and thus they sinned by disobeying him (Genesis 3). Now every human ever born (besides Jesus) has inherited Adam and Eve's sinful nature. The sinful nature is the source of all the evil desires and corruption within humans. Unlike humankind's first parents (Adam and Eve) who sinned and then became sinful, now the Bible explains that we all sin because we are born sinful (Psalm 51:5, Romans 5:19, Romans 3:23).

The penalty for sin is death (Romans 6:23). Because sin has corrupted the entire human race, death, chaos, and all kinds of evil are all around us.

We were created to be born into a perfect world, but because of sin we are born into a corrupted world. We were created to have perfect parents, families, and health, but because of sin we have flawed parents, flawed families, and fading health at best. We were created to have purpose and meaning, but because of sin we are lost and aimlessly drifting in our lives. We were created to worship God in an intimate relationship, but now because of sin, from the moment we are born we do not know God and we live for ourselves rather than for him.

We all know there's a problem, and so throughout our whole lives we will be looking for a solution, looking for ways to feel better. You may have thought a relationship, money, fame, drugs, gambling, a healthy body, sex, or numerous other things could fill the hole inside of you. None of it has worked because the source of our problems is that our relationship with God is broken. Only when this relationship is restored will the rest of our life make any sense.

In summary, humans are designed to be loved by God and to love God. Sin ruined this relationship. We have all searched for wholeness in many places, but until we find God nothing will work. We will always feel empty until we regain what we lost through sin – a right relationship with God.

The gospel is God's solution to the problem of sin. The word gospel means "good news." It is a word that summarizes God's solution to the "bad news" caused by sin that we see all around us. Through the gospel, all our sins are wiped away (forgiveness), our relationship with God is restored, we are filled with God's love, and we are given power to love God (expressed in obedience) as he originally wanted.

This is the gospel: God sent his one and only Son to die on the cross for our sins. God raised Jesus from the dead, conquering death, and has now given everyone the opportunity to receive a new life in Christ. We receive this forgiveness and newness by grace and through faith in Jesus. (1 Corinthians 15:1-4, Ephesians 2:8-9)

We were born sinful and throughout our lives we sinned in many ways; therefore we all need to be "born again" so we can have the ability to love, obey, and reflect God as he originally wanted. The gospel is the solution to the world's problems and to our individual issues as well. Only through the gospel can true and lasting transformation take place.

Questions:

1. Where have you searched for love and wholeness? Did you find what you were looking for?

2. In the beginning of this chapter, you were asked, "Why do you think there are so many problems in the world?" Explain how the Bible answers this question.

Why Is the Gospel So Important?

Imagine walking into a classroom where the kids are running around, throwing paper, and pushing one another. The sound from screaming kids is deafening. Tables and desks are rocking as kids jump and dance on them. "What is going on here?" you wonder. Suddenly you realize there is no teacher in the room. The kids have gone completely bonkers because they have been left to their own devices. Would you really expect kids to act any different without adult supervision?

In a much more serious and fatal way, this is what our world has become when humans ignore God. But our Teacher has not left us, rather we as the students have ignored God (sin) and therefore our world and our individual lives are in chaos. When we do not follow God and his instructions, everything gets out of order.

The gospel is key for transformation because through the gospel our connection with God is restored. Like a teacher to a classroom, God brings order, direction, and counsel to our lives. Perhaps more accurately, like parents to a child, when our relationship with God is restored we receive the love, comfort, direction, and strength we've been looking for our whole lives.

When God is not in control of our lives, Ephesians 2:1-3 explains that there are three very bad influences that try to control our lives in place of God:

> *Once you were dead because of your disobedience and your many sins. ² You used to live in sin, just like the rest of the world, obeying the devil—the commander of the powers in the unseen world. He is the spirit at work in the hearts of those who refuse to obey God. ³ All of us used to live that way, following the passionate desires and inclinations of our sinful nature. By our very nature we were subject to God's anger, just like everyone else.*

Every human has three enemies working against them: the sinful nature (the flesh), the world, and the devil.

- The sinful nature is the sin living in us that leads us away from God through evil desires. Every human inherited this from Adam and Eve.

- The "world" is the sinful systems and evil ways of living the masses participate in. "Worldliness" is similar to "godlessness." If we disobey God, we are living a "worldly" life. When we follow the masses who do not love God, we are dragged away by the world.

- Satan is a fallen angel who leads legions of demons who have the power to tempt us into sin and away from God.

Although we are responsible for our own choices, all three of these evil influences lead us into sin. The result of sin is death because sin cuts us off from the source of life (God). Without God, our behavior is shaped by these three evil influences. If we are left in our sins without the help of God, we are doomed. Thankfully God does offer help to us. Ephesians 2:4-7 states:

> *4But God is so rich in mercy, and he loved us so much, 5 that even though we were dead because of our sins, he gave us life when he raised Christ from the dead. (It is only by God's grace that you have been saved!) 6 For he raised us from the dead along with Christ and seated us with him in the heavenly realms because we are united with Christ Jesus.7 So God can point to us in all future ages as examples of the incredible wealth of his grace and kindness toward us, as shown in all he has done for us who are united with Christ Jesus.*

We were dead in our sins, but God sent Jesus to die on the cross and be raised from the dead so that we could be forgiven and alive with him. Transformation can now take place because the source of our problems is now defeated. God defeated these three enemies by making us alive with Christ.

God gives us a new nature through Christ with new desires so we can please God rather than our sinful nature (Ephesians 4:20-24). God has made us a member of his family so we no longer need to be a part of the world (Ephesians 2:6). Through the gospel God has given us power to resist the devil so he will flee from us (Ephesians 6:10-11).

Through the gospel transformation is now possible. We use to be dead in our sins as we followed our flesh, the world, and the devil (Ephesians 2:1-3). But now we have the opportunity to follow God. Because he loves us he sent his Son, Jesus Christ, to free us from all evil and to give us the ability to love and follow him (Ephesians 2:4-7).

In summary, God designed us to live for him. The flesh, the world, and the devil tempt us to live for ourselves and worship false gods (drugs, lust, greed, gluttony, selfishness, etc.). Our sin has broken our relationship with God and thus chaos has occurred in our lives and in the world. Only through the gospel is our sin wiped away, we are given a new nature eager to please God, and thus our relationship with God is restored. Only when we are reconnected with God will we find transformation and happiness. C.S. Lewis put it like this:

> "God made us: invented us as a man invents an engine. A car is made to run on gas, and it would not run properly on anything else. Now God designed the human machine to run on Himself. He Himself is the fuel our spirits were designed to burn, or the food our spirits were designed to feed on. There is no other. That is why it is just no good asking God to make us happy in our own way without bothering about religion. God cannot give

us a happiness and peace apart from Himself,
because it is not there."

<u>Questions:</u>

1. Who is happier more often, a child with parents who discipline her often or a child who can do whatever she wants? Why? What insights can you apply from this to your relationship with God?

2. Read Ephesians 2:1-7. Summarize these verses in your own words. (If you need help doing this, answer these two questions: What was the problem mentioned in verses 1-3? What was the solution mentioned in verses 4-7?)

How Can You Receive the Gospel?

Have you ever seen the movie *Saving Private Ryan*? It's a story that takes place during World War II, right as the US is trying to take back France from German control. A group of valiant soldiers are sent by a General to find one man, Private Ryan, who is behind enemy lines. The US soldiers struggle through traps set by the enemy, landmines are everywhere, enemy snipers are picking them off, and some of the soldiers die in their search for Private Ryan.

Eventually these mighty men find him after a grueling, sacrificial search. But rather than leave his post, Private Ryan wants to stay in the fight and help win the war. The US soldiers sent to save him decide to stay and help him complete his mission.

In much the same way, this story is reminiscent of how God sent Jesus for us. God sent Jesus to come and save us as we are trapped behind enemy lines. But unlike the General who wanted Private Ryan to leave the fight and come home, God expects us to do what Private Ryan did. God did not just send Jesus so we can live the same life now but go to heaven one day. God sent Jesus so we could be successful in the fight now and spend eternity with him forever. God has a mission for each of us, and only through the power God sends to us through Jesus will we be able to successfully accomplish it.

But what if when the US soldiers found Private Ryan, he told them to go away, that he did not need their help? What if he refused to accept the General's offer of future safety from the war and the soldier's offer of additional help during the battle? Sadly, this is often what humans do when we refuse to receive the gift of the gospel that God has sent to us through Jesus Christ.

So how can we receive the gospel? How can we make sure we will live forever with God when this war is over while also living with power now as we complete the mission he has given us on earth? Ephesians 2:8-10 gives us the answer:

> *8 God saved you by his grace when you believed. And you can't take credit for this; it is a gift from God. 9 Salvation is not a reward for the good things we have done, so none of us can boast about it. 10 For we are God's masterpiece. He has created us anew in Christ Jesus, so we can do the good things he planned for us long ago.*

Grace is a gift we don't deserve. It is God's offer of salvation, redemption, and transformation through the power of Jesus Christ. If you receive something that you earned through your own character, good choices, or hard work, this is not grace. Grace is totally dependent on God's love for us and not our love for God. The Bible says we are saved "by grace" and "not by works." To receive the gospel, we must first accept that everything God offers us is "by grace."

Faith is believing God so much that you live differently because of your trust in him. Hebrews 11:1 says, "Now faith is confidence in what we hope for and assurance about what we do not see." Even though we can't see God right now, even though we did not see Jesus die and rise from the dead, God still expects us to have faith in these truths. When we have faith in God, it is like cashing the check God has already written for us. To receive the gospel we must accept that everything God offers us is "by grace" and received "through faith."

Good works are the deeds God wants us to do for him. We are not saved by doing good works. But when we are saved "by grace" and "through faith" our "good works" will be a sign of our salvation (James 2:14-18). When we truly put our faith in God, our lives will look different as we are empowered by his grace. We will not live a perfect life, but we will have "good works" present in our lives as the evidence of our conversion. To receive the gospel we must accept that everything God offers is "by grace," "through faith," and now we must live for God as his "handiwork, created in Christ Jesus to do good works, which God prepared in advance for us to do."

God is offering you the chance to be transformed. He sent his Son to save us from our sins, to give us a new nature, and help us live for God now and forever. God desires for your relationship with him to be restored. Nothing will bring wholeness, healing, love, or transformation except a restored relationship with God.

Perhaps you have never put your faith in Jesus Christ. Or perhaps you once put your faith in Jesus Christ in the past, but since that time you have backslidden and have not followed God with all your heart. Do you want your sins to be forgiven? Do you want a new nature? Would you like a restored relationship with God?

You can have all of this by God's grace if you put your faith in Jesus Christ, repent of your sin, and dedicate the rest of your life to following him. If you would like to receive God's offer of salvation and transformation, or if you would like to rededicate your life to God, here is a prayer to help guide you. This prayer is not magical. You can pray your own words to God. But if you don't know what to say but want to be in a relationship with God, this prayer is meant to help guide you:

Dear God,
Thank you for sending your Son, Jesus Christ. I believe he died on the cross for my sins and was raised from the dead on the third day. I put my faith in Jesus and ask you to save me, restore my relationship with you, and transform me completely. I confess all of my sins and I thank you for cleansing me completely through the blood of Jesus. I repent of my former way of life and choose to now live for you. I believe your gift of salvation is all by grace. Thank you for saving me. Please help me to now grow in my relationship with you, follow you for my whole life, to

always repent and ask for forgiveness when I sin, and help me to seek to please you in everything I do. In Jesus name I pray, amen.

1. Define the word "grace" in your own words. Have you ever been shown grace in your life?

2. God saves us *from* our sins, the flesh, the world, and the devil. But what does God save us *for*?

Reflection Questions:

1. What's your history with God? Do you believe in him? What good and bad experiences have you had in relation to Christianity?

2. Where do you commonly look for pleasure, happiness, and love? Do you think these things will fill you? Why or why not?

3. Have you tried to change areas of your life before? What have you tried to change, how did you try to change, and what were the results?

4. Are you ready to receive God's gift of salvation offered through the gospel? Why or why not? If you are a Christian, what part of your life would you like to change so you can follow God better?

Getting Started: A.W. Tozer said, "What comes into our minds when we think about God is the most important thing about us." How do you feel about this quote? Do you agree or disagree? Explain your answer.

Who Is God and What Is He Like?

A.W. Tozer said, "What comes into our minds when we think about God is the most important thing about us." So who is God and what is he really like? As we will see in this chapter, our answers to these questions will shape the way we live.

Jesus told us a story in Matthew 25:14-30 to drive home this point. In this parable (which is a fictional story used to teach a lesson) Jesus described a rich man who had three servants. The man was going away on a trip, but before he left he gave each of his servants some money. The first servant and second servant both invested the money. When the rich man came back, he was pleased with their behavior and blessed them with even more of his money to manage.

The third servant, however, did not invest the money. So when the rich man came back from his trip, he was not pleased with this servant's behavior. Why did the two servants behave in a pleasing way to the rich man while the third servant acted in a displeasing way? We find the answer in Matthew 25:24-25:

> *"Then the servant with the one bag of silver came and said, 'Master, I knew you were a harsh man, harvesting crops you didn't plant and gathering crops you didn't cultivate.* [25] *I was afraid I would lose your money, so I hid it in the earth. Look, here is your money back.'"*

This third servant who acted badly had a very bad view of this rich man. His poor beliefs about his master led to poor behavior towards his master. The other servants had a better understanding of the rich man, therefore their behavior was better. Jesus is helping us all understand why our beliefs about God are so important. How we view God will shape how we act towards God in our lives.

So how can we know the truth? Who is God and what is God really like? The answer to these questions are found in the Bible. As 1 John 4:1-3 explains, there are many false ideas out there about God. Ultimately, we will know what is true by testing it against what the Bible says:

> *"Dear friends, do not believe everyone who claims to speak by the Spirit. You must test them to see if the spirit they have comes from God. For there are many false prophets in the world.* [2] *This is how we know if they have the Spirit of God: If a person claiming to be a prophet acknowledges that Jesus Christ came in a real body, that person has the Spirit of God.* [3] *But if someone claims to be a prophet and does not acknowledge the truth about Jesus, that person is not from God. Such a person has the spirit of the Antichrist, which you heard is coming into the world and indeed is already here."*

So who is God? As this passage of Scripture shows us, God is one while also being three different persons. The Father, Son, and Holy Spirit are all mentioned here. This is called the Trinity. The Father is often just referred to as "God."

The Father plans what is going to happen (John 6:38, Acts 1:7). The Son is Jesus Christ. He accomplishes the Father's plan, reveals the Father to us, obeys the Father, and rules with the Father (Hebrews 1:1-3, John 6:38. John 17:4-5). The Holy Spirit applies what the Son has accomplished. The Holy Spirit enters into Christians at the moment they put their faith in Jesus and gives them every spiritual blessing possible (Ephesians 1:3, 13-14, Acts 1:8).

Throughout the Bible, God is described in many ways. He is called the loving Father while also being the just Judge. He is like a kind nursing mother, but he is also like a mighty warrior who defends his people. God is a close friend to those who have put their faith in him while also being the King of the universe seated on the throne in heaven. As you can see, although God is simply Father, Son, and Holy Spirit, God expresses his character in many different ways throughout the Bible.

So if you had to summarize what God was like in the simplest way possible, it would be fair to use just two words: love and holy. Love is doing what's best for someone at great cost to yourself. Jesus said that the highest form of love is to lay down your life for a friend (John 15:13). 1 John 4:9-10 explains how the Father showed his love for us:

> *9 God showed how much he loved us by sending his one and only Son into the world so that we might have eternal life through him. 10 This is real love— not that we loved God, but that he loved us and sent his Son as a sacrifice to take away our sins.*

The reason Jesus had to pay for our sins with his own blood was because God is holy. To be holy means to be perfect in every way, set apart from common use, and to be without any blemish or sin. God is so holy that no amount of sin or imperfection can come into his presence. He judges all wrong doing, from the smallest evil thought to the worst crimes ever committed, because he is perfectly holy.

God loves us but because God is holy, our sin has separated us from God. So God sent Jesus to make us holy and bring us into a relationship with him. When we put our faith in the gospel, God makes each of us into a holy person who is now a part of a holy nation (1 Peter 2:9).

So why is knowing about the holiness and love of God key for transformation? If you only understand the holiness of God, you might feel distant from him and constantly ashamed of your sin since all humans are unholy without the gospel. If you only understand the love of God, you might assume God cares about you so much that he can look past your sins and that you can have a relationship with God regardless of your sinfulness.

Because God is so holy, he can never look past any sin. But because God loves us so much, he makes us holy through the blood of Jesus when we put our faith in Christ.

<u>Questions:</u>

1. Why is it important that we have a true understanding of who God really is?

2. How would you describe God? Why do you describe him this way?

Why Is It Important to Know Who God Is and What He Is Like?

Take a moment and think about the times in life when you have hurt those you love. It's not pleasant to remember these times, but it can motivate us to change. Don't you want to love people better, to have more patience, to have more self-control, and to be a more reliable friend and family member? Our success and failure in our most important relationships depends on our walk with God.

This can be seen right at the beginning of our human story. Adam and Eve fell to the temptations of Satan and ate from the tree that God told them not to eat. But how did Satan deceive Adam and Eve? He corrupted their beliefs about God. Genesis 3:1-6 says:

> *The serpent was the shrewdest of all the wild animals the Lord God had made. One day he asked the woman, "Did God really say you must not eat the fruit from any of the trees in the garden?"*
>
> *² "Of course we may eat fruit from the trees in the garden," the woman replied. ³ "It's only the fruit from the tree in the middle of the garden that we are not allowed to eat. God said, 'You must not eat it or even touch it; if you do, you will die.'"*
>
> *⁴ "You won't die!" the serpent replied to the woman. ⁵ "God knows that your eyes will be opened as soon as you eat it, and you will be like God, knowing both good and evil."*
>
> *⁶ The woman was convinced. She saw that the tree was beautiful and its fruit looked delicious, and she wanted the wisdom it would give her. So she took some of the fruit and ate it. Then she gave some to her husband, who was with her, and he ate it, too.*

Adam and Eve started to live a sinful life as soon as their beliefs about God became untrue. Satan tempted them to believe that God was keeping this fruit from them because he did not want them to be like God. This was a lie, but when Adam and Eve believed this lie, they started to behave sinfully. When we believe lies about God, our behavior will become evil too. Satan knew that if he could get them to believe the worst about God, then sin was not far behind. What we believe about God will shape our behavior. A.W. Tozer states:

> "What comes into our minds when we think about God is the most important thing about us. For this reason the most serious question before the Church is always God Himself, and the most significant fact about any man is not what he at a given time may say or do, but what he in his deep heart thinks God like. We often live by a secret law of the soul that moves us toward our mental image of God."

When you really believe that God is holy, you will pursue holiness yourself in Christ. Notice how 1 Peter 1:15-16 puts it:

> *15 But now you must be holy in everything you do, just as God who chose you is holy. 16 For the Scriptures say, "You must be holy because I am holy."*

To be holy, we must first recognize and believe that God is holy. Our belief about God will shape our own behavior. People are like arrows. We are always moving towards what we are looking at. If you are looking at a false picture of God, you will start living a sinful life. 1 John 4:7-13 explains that when we know the God of love, our life will show love.

> *"Beloved, let us love one another, for love is from God, and whoever loves has been born of God and knows God. 8 Anyone who does not love does not know God, because God is love. 9 In this the love of God was made manifest among us, that God sent his only Son into the world, so that we might live*

through him. ¹⁰ In this is love, not that we have loved God but that he loved us and sent his Son to be the propitiation for our sins. ¹¹ Beloved, if God so loved us, we also ought to love one another.¹² No one has ever seen God; if we love one another, God abides in us and his love is perfected in us.

¹³ By this we know that we abide in him and he in us, because he has given us of his Spirit."

Transformation happens when we are connected to the true power source. When we are filled with God, we are then filled with love, and then we can act lovingly.

God acts the way he does because of his identity. Who God is shapes what God does. Likewise, we too live from our identity. What we do flows from who we are. When we were not a part of the family of God, we lived a lifestyle that followed our sinful nature, the world, and the devil. 1 John 3:9-10 says:

No one born of God makes a practice of sinning, for God's seed abides in him; and he cannot keep on sinning, because he has been born of God. ¹⁰ By this it is evident who are the children of God, and who are the children of the devil: whoever does not practice righteousness is not of God, nor is the one who does not love his brother.

When our identity is rooted in Christ, then we are free to love and act how we want rather than to be controlled by the false gods of our past (people, drugs, money, Etc.).

<u>Questions:</u>

1. How would you summarize why Adam and Eve disobeyed God?

2. 1 John 4:8 says, "Anyone who does not love does not know God, because God is love." Explain in your own words what this means. Give a real life example of this verse in action.

How Can We Know God and Love God?

How can we know and love God? It's the right question to ask because according to the Bible, knowing God comes first and love will flow out of what we know about God. 1 John 4:14-21 says this:

> *14 And we have seen and testify that the Father has sent his Son to be the Savior of the world. 15 Whoever confesses that Jesus is the Son of God, God abides in him, and he in God. 16 So we have come to know and to believe the love that God has for us. God is love, and whoever abides in love abides in God, and God abides in him. 17 By this is love perfected with us, so that we may have confidence for the day of judgment, because as he is so also are we in this world. 18 There is no fear in love, but perfect love casts out fear. For fear has to do with punishment, and whoever fears has not been perfected in love. 19 We love because he first loved us. 20 If anyone says, "I love God," and hates his brother, he is a liar; for he who does not love his brother whom he has seen cannot love God whom he has not seen. 21 And this commandment we have from him: whoever loves God must also love his brother.*

Verses 14-15 say that when we see God accurately we will be bold for God in our lives. Verses 16-18 says that when we know and believe the love God has for us we will begin to live a life of love without any fear. Lastly, verses 19-21 say that we will love God when we truly accept the truth that God loved us first. And when we know that God loves us and we love him in return, this will empower us to love other people too.

In summary, 1 John 4 teaches us that God reveals himself through Jesus Christ (1 John 4:9-10). God showed his love for each one of us through the death and resurrection of Jesus Christ. When we put our faith in Jesus, the Holy

Spirit enters our heart and opens our eyes to the truth about God (1 John 4:13). The more accurately we begin to know God and the closer we draw to him in a personal relationship, the more our life will be radically transformed (1 John 4:19-21).

1. After studying 1 John 4, how would you describe who God is and what he is like?

2. In your own words, describe what you think "holy" means. Describe what "love" means.

Reflection Questions:

1. Pick one Bible verse from this chapter that you found interesting. Copy it here.

2. Why do you like this Bible verse and what has it taught you?

3. How can you make sure your understanding of God is true?

4. Do you tend to emphasize God's love or his holiness more often? Why is it important to remember both the love and holiness of God?

Getting Started: Why do you think God created us? What is our purpose?

Who Is Jesus and What Did He Come to Do?

Imagine you woke up one morning and you were in the middle of the ocean on a ship with other crew members. No one knows how you all got there. No one knows what you all are supposed to be doing. You are all just there . . . on a ship . . . with no coordinates . . . no mission . . . in the middle of the vast ocean.

To make matters worse, no one on the ship really knows anything about sailing, navigating, or fishing. All the equipment for survival and a successful mission are present on the ship, it's just that no one really knows how to use any of this.

After the initial shock begins to wear off, people start taking charge. A lot of mistakes are happening. Some people are getting injured as they try to learn how to operate the ship and use the fishing gear. And of course there is a ton of disagreement. Some people want to sail that way, others want to sail this way. Some want to lower the nets over there to catch fish, others want to drop the nets over here. People start blaming one another for drinking too much of the fresh water. Irritation is rising as food supplies dwindle.

Now imagine a totally different scenario. You are a sailor in service to the king. He has commissioned you to sail across the ocean to explore new lands. Before the voyage your captain teaches you everything you need to know for the mission ahead. When you set sail, the captain is your example, your leader, and is telling you everything you need to know. The mission is difficult but also rewarding. It's a success. The king is pleased with you on your return and he honors you for your faithful service.

These two scenarios could not be more different. In the first scene you are confused, directionless, untrained, and you don't even know why you are at sea to begin with. In the second scene you have a clear purpose and you have a captain leading you on a successful mission.

The first scene is how most of us go through life before we come to know Jesus Christ and discover our true purpose. Before the truth of God's word is revealed to us, we know we are here on earth, we know we are supposed to be doing something, we all try to survive the best we can, but overall it's pretty much a huge, dangerous mess.

But when we start reading the Bible and accepting it as truth, direction is given and things start making sense. Jesus is like our captain. He shows us what the Father's mission is for us. The Holy Spirit empowers us for the voyage ahead. And God sails with us for the whole journey, through all the ups and downs.

So who is Jesus and what did he come to earth to do? When we can successfully answer this question, we will know our purpose as well and we will be given the strength to accomplish it.

The Bible is the only place to turn if you really want to know who Jesus is. There are many amazing passages of Scripture that teach us much about Jesus. Perhaps some of the most helpful verses about who Jesus is are found in Philippians 2:6-8:

> *Though he was God,he did not think of equality with Godas something to cling to.[7] Instead, he gave up his divine privileges; he took the humble position of a slaveand was born as a human being.When he appeared in human form,[8] he humbled himself in obedience to Godand died a criminal's death on a cross.*

Core to Jesus identity are the facts that Jesus is fully God and fully man. Jesus has always been as God is, which means Jesus is God and has existed as God eternally before creation. However, Jesus was also conceived by the Holy Spirit as a human in the womb of Mary at a specific time in history. Jesus really became a man in flesh and blood. That's who Jesus is – both fully God and fully man. But what did he come to earth to do? Philippians 2:9-11explains:

> *Therefore, God elevated him to the place of highest honorand gave him the name above all other names,[10] that at the name of Jesus every knee should bow,in heaven and on earth and under the earth,[11] and every tongue declare that Jesus Christ is Lord, to the glory of God the Father.*

Jesus came to earth to set prisoners free, heal the sick, give sight to the blind, and offer eternal life and transformation to all humans. He came to die on the cross and be raised from the dead. He came to preach the good news. All of this is true. But why did he do all these things?

There are many answers we can give here, but they all can get boiled down to one answer. Ultimately, Jesus Christ came to earth to glorify God. Because of Jesus, "every tongue [will] declare that Jesus Christ is Lord, to the glory of God the Father" (Philippians 2:11).

What is the glory of God? The Bible uses this phrase in many different ways, which means we can create many different definitions in general. However, the Bible primarily uses the phrase "the glory of God" in a specific way, and therefore what follows is a specific definition. The glory of God is the invisible qualities, character, or attributes of God displayed in a visible (or knowable) way.

Isaiah 6:2 states, "Holy, holy, holy is the LORD of hosts; the whole earth is full of his glory!" You'd think this verse would end by saying, "the whole earth is full of his holiness." But it doesn't. It states that the whole earth is full of God's glory. When the character of God, like his holiness, goes public for the world to witness and know, the Bible refers to this as "God's glory."

When the Israelites were rescued from Egypt and God led them by a cloud in the day and a cloud of fire by night, the Bible states "the glory of the LORD appeared" (Exodus 16:7-10). Obviously the glory of God is not a cloud or fireball. But when the character or quality of God is displayed publicly like it was in this example, the Bible refers to this as "the glory of God."

When Moses was on the top of Mount Sinai speaking with God, "Moses said, 'Please show me your glory.' And [God] said, 'I will make all my goodness pass before you and will proclaim before you my name 'The LORD'" (Exodus 33:18-19). Again, the glory of God is the invisible character of God displayed. So when God visibly showed Moses his goodness and allowed Moses to know and understand the proclamation of God's name "The LORD," this was the same thing as God showing his glory to Moses.

God created the universe, the stars, the world, and everything, and it all bears God's image to some degree. Thus the Bible states that all creation declares God's glory (Psalm 19:1-4, Romans 1:20-23).

Humans were made for the glory of God (Isaiah 43:7). Therefore God made humans in the image of God (Genesis 1:27).

Lastly, Jesus glorifies God the most because he reveals God the most because he is God in the flesh. Humans are made *in* God's image, but Jesus *is* God's image (John 1:1, John 1:14, 2 Corinthians 4:4-6, Colossians 1:15, Hebrews 1:3).

In summary, when we read Philippians 2:6-11, we see that Jesus is fully God and fully man, that he came to earth to die on the cross, and he did all this "to the glory of God the Father" (Philippians 2:11).

Questions:

1. How do you feel (list the emotions) when you are lost and running late to an important event? Now,how do you feel when you are with someone who knows where you are going even if you have never been there before?

2. Describe in your own words who Jesus is, what he came to do, and why he came to do it?

Why Is Jesus So Important to Our Transformation and Purpose?

The shortest way to summarize the previous section is this: Jesus came to earth to glorify the Father through loving and saving people.

Why is this so important for us to know? Throughout the pages of Scripture, we are told that Jesus is our example in everything (John 13:14-15, Ephesians 5:1-2). He is the perfect human because he is also our perfect God. If Jesus' mission and purpose on earth was to glorify God through loving him and other people (John 17:1-5), it's logical to assume this is also our purpose too. It's not only logical, but this is exactly what the Bible plainly tells us. Philippians 2:1-5explains:

> *Is there any encouragement from belonging to Christ? Any comfort from his love? Any fellowship together in the Spirit? Are your hearts tender and compassionate?² Then make me truly happy by agreeing wholeheartedly with each other, loving one another, and working together with one mind and purpose.*
>
> *³ Don't be selfish; don't try to impress others. Be humble, thinking of others as better than yourselves.⁴ Don't look out only for your own interests, but take an interest in others, too.*
>
> *⁵ You must have the same attitude that Christ Jesus had.*

Again, Philippians 2:5 says, "You must have the same attitude that Christ Jesus had." Our purpose on earth is the same as Jesus Christ's purpose: to love other people, to put others above ourselves, and to imitate Jesus in the way we live.

Why is this our purpose? Because God designed us to glorify him. Remember, to glorify means to reveal, to shed light on, to exalt, or to make visible. Jesus revealed God through his sacrificial love for humans. Our mission and purpose in life is to bear God's image. We were made to worship and bring him praise by reflecting him in everything we do. And we reflect him best when we love God, love people, and act like Jesus.

Jesus is so important to our transformation for at least two reasons. 1. He is the example we are to follow. 2. He empowers us to do God's will.

If our purpose is to bear God's image, we must first know what God looks and acts like if we are to imitate him. Jesus came to show us this very thing. He came to reveal God to us:

> *Christ became human flesh and lived among us. We saw His shining- greatness (glory). This greatness is given only to a much-loved Son from His Father. He was full of loving-favor and truth. . . .[18] The much-loved Son is beside the Father. No man has ever seen God. But Christ has made God known to us.(John 1:14, 18 NLV)*

Because of Jesus, we now know how we are to live. But God not only shows us what our lives should like in Jesus, he also empowers us for this purpose through Jesus as well:

> *[29]For God knew his people in advance, and he chose them to become like his Son, so that his Son would be the firstborn among many brothers and sisters. [30] And having chosen them, he called them to come to him. And having called them, he gave them right standing with himself. And having given them right standing, <u>he gave them his glory</u>.(Romans 8:29-30)*

In summary, our mission is to love God, love people, and to do it all for the glory God. We accomplish this mission by living like Christ through the glory God gives us.

Questions:

1. What are the two ways Jesus helps us accomplish our purpose?

2. Why do you think it glorifies God when we love other people?

How Can You Live Like Christ?

To live like Christ we must know Christ intimately and rely on him only. Philippians 2:12-13explains:

> *[12] Dear friends, you always followed my instructions when I was with you. And now that I am away, it is even more important. Work hard to show the results of your salvation, obeying God with deep reverence and fear. [13] For God is working in you, giving you the desire and the power to do what pleases him.*

If you were to read Philippians 2:13 in isolation, you would have a desire to argue that if it is God who sovereignly works in us to give us both the desire and the power to obey him, then why are we responsible when we disobey God?

However, when you read Philippians 2:12 and 13 together, this logic is turned on its head. God's power in us is the reason we should act rightly, not an excuse to not act rightly. We are told to obey God. Why? "For it is God who works in you . . . ." God's power in us is why God now expects us to obey him.

It's true that "it all depends on God," but only in the context of our good actions, not in the context of our decision to do something or not. The fact that God is the source behind all good should never be used as freedom from personally making sure good is done. Rather, the fact that God is the source behind all good should empower and embolden our right behavior and decision because we know he lives in us if we have put our faith in Jesus.

Therefore, to live like Jesus, we must do at least two things: work hard and believe God is working in you. Philippians 2:12-13 tells us to do both of these things. We are not told to work hard to be saved but rather because we are saved. When we believe verse 13, we will be empowered to accomplish verse 12.

Questions:

1.Summarize Philippians 2:12 in your own words.

2. Summarize Philippians 2:13 in your own words

Reflection Questions:

1. After reading this chapter, has your understanding of what your purpose is changed at all? Why or why not?

2. Have you ever had a mentor, coach, or parent/guardian teach you how to do something you could not have done on your own? How did this make you feel?

3. According to the Bible, who is Jesus? According to the Bible, why did Jesus come to earth?

4. If you want to live like Jesus and be led by him, what do you personally need to stop doing and what do you need to start doing?

Week 4
You Are Free (Justification)
Key Text: Galatians 2:16-21

Getting Started: If you are in massive financial debt, how does this affect your life? How would it feel to have all the debt erased? How would life be different with the debt compared to life without the debt?

What Is Justification? What Has Gone Done to Us Through Christ?

A man was summoned to court because he had neglected to pay his taxes for many years. He now owed such an immense debt he could never pay it back. Just as the judge was about to throw the man into prison, an unexpected turn of events happened.

The man had an advocate. His older brother suddenly volunteered to pay the entire debt on behalf of the man. The judge was suspicious at first. But it all checked out. The debt was paid in full and therefore the man was released.

In the eyes of the law, this man was now totally free and had no criminal record. He had done wrong. He had lived an irresponsible life. He had incurred massive debt. His own deeds deserved prison time. But because of the actions of his advocate, the judge pronounced the man free and innocent.

This is what Jesus does for us. In the eyes of the Judge, we are guilty without Christ. We stand before him with a debt so large we can never pay it back. The just thing is for us to be in prison for eternity. But Jesus steps in and pays the debt for us.

Now, what if this person in our story after leaving the court started making payments on his old debt anyway? He works every day, all day, seven days a week, desperately trying to pay the amount he had previously owed. He is actually free in the eyes of the law. But the way this man lives, it's as though he is still imprisoned by the law.

This is what it's like when Christians start trying to have a right relationship with God through obedience to the law rather than through faith in Jesus. When we are offered salvation through faith and by grace, but we then try to have a right relationship with God through obeying the law, we are choosing to be condemned by the very thing we were rescued from. The only way to be right with God is through embracing our justification given to us through Jesus Christ. Galatians 2:16 says:

> *Yet we know that a person is made right with God [justified] by faith in Jesus Christ, not by obeying the law. And we have believed in Christ Jesus, so that we might be made right with God [justified] because of our faith in Christ, not because we have obeyed the law. For no one will ever be made right with God [justified] by obeying the law."*

Justification is a legal term that means someone is declared innocent of past crimes. Jesus justified us by imparting his innocence to us. God laid our sin on Jesus when he was on the cross and then God laid Jesus' righteousness on us when we believed. 2 Corinthians 5:21 "God made him who had no sin to be sin for us, so that in him we might become the righteousness of God."

Justification refers to our eternal position in Christ. You've been given Christ's purity, Christ's righteousness, Christ's love, Christ's perfection. When God looks at you, God sees the perfect qualities of Christ because God imparted those perfections to us through faith. Warren Wiersbe said, "Justification is not a process; it is an act. It is not something the sinner does; it is something God does for the sinner when he puts his faith in Christ. It is a once-for-all event. It never changes." Galatians 3:10-12 says:

> But those who depend on the law to make them right with God are under his curse, for the Scriptures say, "Cursed is everyone who does not observe and obey all the commands that are written in God's Book of the Law." [11] So it is clear that no one can be made right with God [justified] by trying to keep the law. For the Scriptures say, "It is through faith that a righteous person has life." [12] This way of faith is very different from the way of law, which says, "It is through obeying the law that a person has life."

When we are justified through faith, we are literally given the purity, holiness, and new nature of Jesus Christ. We can never be declared perfect by God through our own actions. You are a new creation if you have put your faith in Jesus. The Holy Spirit enters into us and gives us the life of Christ (Galatians 3:1-5).

<u>Questions:</u>

1. What does the word "justification" mean?

2. Why is it so tempting to try and be made right with God through obeying the law?

Why Is Justification So Important for Transformation?

> *But suppose we seek to be made right with God*
> *[justified] through faith in Christ and then we are*
> *found guilty because we have abandoned the law.*
> *Would that mean Christ has led us into sin?*
> *Absolutely not! 18 Rather, I am a sinner if I rebuild*
> *the old system of law I already tore down. 19 For*
> *when I tried to keep the law, it condemned me. So I*
> *died to the law—I stopped trying to meet all its*
> *requirements—so that I might live for God.*
> *(Galatians 2:17-19)*

When we become a Christian, we often think we are getting a "second chance" at obeying the law. We think, "Now I'm really going to get it right!" But this is not the point of Christianity. This is not our second chance to live by obeying the law. Rather, Christ fulfilled the requirements of the law for us. Now we must learn to live by faith in Christ.

The "second chance" mentality is not accurate. The amount of chances we have had is not the problem. If you were given another chance with your same old self, everything would turn out the same because your spiritual condition is the same and our spiritual condition is what determines our actions.

Rather than give us a second chance, God justifies us and gives a sure thing. You are perfectly holy, pure, and new because God has transferred the life of Christ into you. By justifying us, God has not only wiped out our debts but has also given us endless resources in our spiritual bank accounts. In an instant, God justified you and gave everything you need for life and godliness:

> *3 By his divine power, God has given us everything*
> *we need for living a godly life. We have received all*
> *of this by coming to know him, the one who called*
> *us to himself by means of his marvelous glory and*
> *excellence. 4 And because of his glory and*
> *excellence, he has given us great and precious*

promises. These are the promises that enable you to share his divine nature and escape the world's corruption caused by human desires. (2 Peter 1:3-4)

At the end of World War I, the victorious countries sought retribution from the losers, especially from Germany. As a way to punish the Germans, the victorious countries created the Treaty of Versailles. This treaty took away lands, profits, certain trading privileges, and much military freedom. It was so costly to the already defeated Germany that through the coming decades the Germans would endure a dark economic depression.

As times grew harder and harder for the German people, they blamed the Treaty of Versailles more and more. Their animosity towards the world grew and they became very welcoming to any rising leaders who would stand up and defy the restrictions placed on them. One leader seemed to capture the hearts of the people like no one else. His stirring speeches played on the peoples' discontentment and empowered them with bold, brash words. As he grew in power, he led the Nationalist Socialist Party towards complete control over all of Germany. Later he transformed this political entity into the Nazi Party. His name was Adolf Hitler.

Most historians agree the penalties placed on Germany after losing World War I were a major contributor to what caused Hitler to rise to power and cause World War II. The people were so desperate to escape the penalties ruining their country, Hitler won their affection as he promised a stronger Germany unwilling to back down to anyone.

When the Germans were again the losers in World War II, in the years to follow US President Truman realized that if strict penalties were placed on Germany once more, Europe as a whole could never recover. He feared in the decades to follow another war caused by discontent Germans may become a real possibility. Instead of penalizing the

Germans and making them open to help from America's enemies, the United States adopted the Marshal Plan. This plan purposefully did not take into account the past faults of Germany but sought only to help them create a different future.

Instead of seeking repayment from an already war-ravished nation, America gave resources to Germany. Instead of inflicting trade restriction, America sought to boost trade revenues in Germany. Instead of trying to totally destroy industry, they encouraged the modernization of German industry. The plan worked! No world WWIII has yet occurred.

Justification is so important because God doesn't only forgive us for the wars we've had with him. He not only pays the debt of our sins. He also deposits eternal blessings into our accounts as well. When God justifies us, he gives us what we need through Christ so we can be loyal to God. Ephesians 1:3 says:

> *All praise to God, the Father of our Lord Jesus Christ, who has blessed us with every spiritual blessing in the heavenly realms because we are united with Christ.*

God not only forgives us for our past sins. He also wants to make sure no future wars happen between us and him ever again. So he blesses us with everything we need right from the start. The Christian life is not ultimately about becoming free. It's about being declared free once and for all and then learning to live from that freedom.

If you are a Christian, you are not fighting for your freedom. You are now fighting from your freedom that was fully given to you at the moment of your conversion. Galatians 5:1 explains:

> *So Christ has truly set us free. Now make sure that you stay free, and don't get tied up again in slavery to the law.*

It says Christ has already set us free. Now because we are free, we must put in the energy and hard work to live free, especially in regards to resisting legalism (which is trying to be made right with God through obeying the law).

If you are a Christian, you are free from sin, free from accusations, free from condemnation, and free forever. (As we will study in the next chapter, sanctification is the process of learning to live free, reflecting the freedom that we already completely possess through Christ.)

Questions:

1. Forgiveness is the first step. But what else does God give us when we become a Christian?

2. Do you think Christianity is a second chance? Why or why not?

How Can You Live From the Justification God Has Given You?

> *My old self has been crucified with Christ. It is no longer I who live, but Christ lives in me. So I live in this earthly body by trusting in the Son of God, who loved me and gave himself for me. [21] I do not treat the grace of God as meaningless. For if keeping the law could make us right with God [justified], then there was no need for Christ to die. (Galatians 2:20-21)*

To really live from the justification God has given you, you must embrace that there is now an old you and a new you (Christ in you). Paul says he now has an "old self." This is another phrase referring to the sinful nature. The person who sinned is no longer you. And not only that, the person who will sin is no longer the true you either. Romans 7:18-20 says:

> *And I know that nothing good lives in me, that is, in my sinful nature. I want to do what is right, but I can't. [19] I want to do what is good, but I don't. I don't want to do what is wrong, but I do it anyway. [20] But if I do what I don't want to do, I am not really the one doing wrong; it is sin living in me that does it.*

There are now two natures battling within your body. They both want control. When you feel the urge to sin or when you do sin, this means the old you has taken over. Freedom comes, however, when you truly realize this is not the real you anymore. The real you is the new you in Christ, for as Paul said, "It is no longer I who live, but Christ who live in me" (Galatians 2:20) and "So I am not the one doing wrong; it is sin living in me that does it" (Romans 7:17).

When you sin, God's justification of you remains because it was based on Christ's actions, not yours. Again, Jesus didn't die to give us a second chance. He died to give us a new life that can never be taken away or stained in any way. When we sin, our enjoyment and experience of God's justification suffers. But we are still righteous before God because of Christ.

Again, even after we sin, we are still a new creation because the perfect grace given to us was not given because of something we did, therefore it cannot be taken away by something we might do (1 Corinthians 1:30-31). Jesus literally transfers his qualities to us (righteousness, holiness, and freedom from sin) and thus we remain with these qualities even after we sin. As Paul wrote, "I no longer count on my own righteousness through obeying the law; rather, I become righteous through faith in Christ. For God's way of making us right with himself depends on faith" (Philippians 3:9).

Justification is what you are positionally in Christ. Sanctification is the holiness and goodness you can witness outwardly in your life. As we will discuss in the next chapter, if your response to justification through faith is a desire to sin more, this means you are probably not truly a Christian. The proper response to justification is a deepening sanctification. In other words, because your purity and right standing with God can never be taken away even if you sin, this now means you have the ability to sin less and less as life goes on, not more and more.

But how? How does justification result in a purer life where you are free to act differently? The answer is found in Galatians 2:20, "My old self has been crucified with Christ. It is no longer I who live, but Christ lives in me. So I live in this earthly body by trusting in the Son of God, who loved me and gave himself for me."

Even though we have two natures in our bodies now (the old and the new/the good and the evil), our true selves will be in control of our bodies when we have active faith in the Son, "So I live in this earthly body by trusting in the Son of God."

So we can try to rebuild the law and try to find salvation through works. We can abuse grace by sinning more because we think we have a free pass now that we are saved by faith and not by works. Or, we can choose the right way. When we are truly justified, we will accept that God has completely wiped away our debts, filled our spiritual bank accounts, and now we will live completely different because of this. We will honor God by knowing what we have is undeserved but also undiminished. Because of God's grace, we can now live honorably for the one who has lavishly blessed us.

Question:

1. Galatians 2:20 says, "My old self has been crucified with Christ. It is no longer I who live, but Christ lives in me. So I live in this earthly body by trusting in the Son of God, who loved me and gave himself for me." How will "trusting in the Son of God" affect your behavior?

2. If God has completely justified us, why do we still sin?

Reflection Questions:

1. What Bible verse from Galatians 2:16-21 is really sticking out to you? Why did you pick this verse?

2. When you sin after you've become a Christian, have you blown your second chance? Why or why not?

3. What's the difference between "fighting for freedom" compared to "fighting from freedom"?

4. What questions do you still have about "justification"?

Getting Started: If God creates us into new creations once we put our faith in Jesus Christ, why do we still sin?

What Is Sanctification?

If God creates us into new creations once we put our faith in Jesus Christ, why do we still sin? And if God's grace is endless, why does it matter if we sin? As we look at Romans 6:1-14, we will see that "sanctification" is the answer to our questions.

Imagine if you had been given a bank account that will never drop to $0 no matter how much you spend. But if we can spend whatever we want, doesn't this mean we can spend irresponsibly with no consequences? Likewise, God's grace can never run out. But if this is the case, doesn't this encourage wild living? Romans 5 concludes with these words:

> *God's law was given so that all people could see how sinful they were. But as people sinned more and more, God's wonderful grace became more abundant. 21 So just as sin ruled over all people and brought them to death, now God's wonderful grace rules instead, giving us right standing with God and*

resulting in eternal life through Jesus Christ our Lord." (Romans 5:20-21)

When Paul wrote these words, he knew what the objections would be. If God's grace just keeps increasing with our sin, does this mean there is no consequence for sin? And if God's grace just keeps covering our sins no matter what we do, doesn't this encourage sinful living? Some went so far to say that since God is glorified through giving his grace, we should sin more so God can glorify himself more by giving us more and more grace.

Paul addresses this false way of thinking in Romans 6. He begins with the question, *"Well then, should we keep on sinning so that God can show us more and more of his wonderful grace?" (Romans 6:1)*. The answer Paul gives in Romans 6:2 is profound. He turns everything on its head and totally reverses the logic of it all. He states, *"Of course not! Since we have died to sin, how can we continue to live in it?" (Romans 6:2).*

The big idea explained in Romans 6 is that because of God's grace imparted to you, this should not be a reason to sin more; this is now actually the reason you should be free from sin. Because I have been permanently justified through faith which cannot be taken away, this should now cause me to live more holy, not less.

Paul is saying that the reason you should be able to live free is because Christ has already set you free. Out of our justification, what Christ has imputed to us, should now flow our sanctification. Justification happens in a moment when you first believe. God transfers the perfections of Christ completely to you and they can never be taken away.

Sanctification, however, is a process that occurs over your whole life. Sanctification is the journey of learning to obey God more and more as you learn to walk in the Spirit. It is the process of learning to live from the new nature God has given you through Jesus Christ.

Justification is done to you. Sanctification includes your choice and will. Sanctification is still a work of the Holy Spirit, but it also includes your personal choices. Justification is when God gives you Christ's perfect holiness; sanctification is when your life becomes holier as you apply the word of God to your life. Justification is what you are positionally in Christ. Sanctification is the holiness and goodness you can witness outwardly in your life. Justification frees us from the damning power of sin for eternity. Sanctification frees us from the reigning power of sin in our lives on earth. Christians are sinless before God because of the gospel (justification), but in their life they will be sinning less and less through the refining work of the Holy Spirit (sanctification).

Romans 6 explains that justification and sanctification are not opposed or conflicting truths in the Bible, they are actually connected and relate to one another. Paul is explaining that our sanctification should now actually flow out of our justification. Because you are justified, you should now be showing the evidence of sanctification. Because you have been given all that you need in Christ, you should be growing bit by bit in your life.

When Paul said, "Well then, should we keep on sinning so that God can show us more and more of his wonderful grace? Of course not! Since we have died to sin, how can we continue to live in it?" (Romans 6:1-2), he is basically saying that if there is no sanctification in your life, you were never truly justified either.

The evidence of your salvation will be expressed in your transformation. If there is no change in your life, it means there was no change to your heart.

Questions:

1. If God's grace will never run out, is this a free pass to sin whenever we feel like it? Why or why not?

2. What is the difference between justification and sanctification?

Why Is Sanctification Important for Transformation?

Without understanding the connection between justification and sanctification, we can error in at least two ways. One, we will think we can do whatever we want since God has completely justified us by grace alone. Because God freely gave us forgiveness and righteousness, we can feel we have a free pass to sin as much as we want.

The other mistake would be to assume that because you still struggle with sin, God has not truly justified you. If you do not understand that sanctification is a process, you will doubt that God has truly made you into a new creation when you still struggle against sin.

Sanctification corrects both of these errors. We do not have a free pass to sin endlessly since God's grace is endless. Why? Because someone who has been truly changed by the Holy Spirit will not live like this. If you are truly made into a new creation, it will show up in your life. Looking for excuses to sin more is not the desire of a true Christian.

However, as we all know, Christians do still sin after God makes them into a new creation. Why? If God changed our hearts, shouldn't we be living perfect lives now? Sanctification corrects this false view because the Bible says Christians are now "being sanctified." For example, Hebrews 10:14 (ESV) explains, "For by a single offering he has perfected for all time those who are being sanctified."

While God changed our identity in a moment, it will take a lifetime to learn to live from that new identity. We will never be sinless until we die and are glorified completely, but while we are on planet earth we will be sinning less. Romans 6:3-7 explains:

> *Or have you forgotten that when we were joined with Christ Jesus in baptism, we joined him in his death? ⁴ For we died and were buried with Christ by baptism. And just as Christ was raised from the*

dead by the glorious power of the Father, now we also may live new lives.

⁵ Since we have been united with him in his death, we will also be raised to life as he was. ⁶ We know that our old sinful selves were crucified with Christ so that sin might lose its power in our lives. We are no longer slaves to sin. ⁷ For when we died with Christ we were set free from the power of sin. (Romans 6:3-7)

So why is sanctification so important for our transformation? Romans 6:1-5 tell us what happened to us when we became a Christian. Now Romans 6:6-7 tell us what should be the result, "We know that our old sinful selves were crucified with Christ *so that sin might lose its power in our lives. We are no longer slaves to sin. For when we died with Christ, we were set free from the power of sin.*"

Because our old selves were crucified with Christ, sin has lost its power in our lives. Notice, however, it does not say that sin has died in us or that the sinful nature no longer exists. It's doesn't say that. It says that because we are justified, we now have the power to fight sin. The true you is no longer the sinful desires you feel in your body. We are set free from sin, so now we have the power to live free even though sin still tries to enslave us.

1. What are ways that we often abuse the grace of God?

2. Read Romans 6:6-7 and explain these verses in your own words. What do they mean to you?

How Can We Be Sanctified?

Ultimately, just like justification, sanctification is the work of the Holy Spirit. But unlike justification, sanctification is contingent upon our personal choices as well. The work of the Holy Spirit and our choices certainly blur together, and while this topic can be mysterious, the Spirit's empowerment of us and our freedom to choose do not contradict.

Notice the emphasis on the words "know" and "believe" throughout Romans 6. Romans 6:3 (NIV), "Or don't you *know* that all of us who were baptized into Christ Jesus were baptized into his death?"Romans 6:6 (NIV), "For we *know* that our old self was crucified with him." Romans 6:8 (NIV), "Now if we died with Christ, we *believe* we will also live with him." And Romans 6:9 (NIV), "For we *know* that since Christ was raised from the dead, he cannot die again."

Paul starts with the mind because our objective and factual beliefs are the foundation for our subjective experiences and feelings. What you experience often stems from what you believe. Your mental beliefs often govern your feelings.

For example: When someone tricks you and makes you believe that a spider is on your head, you can feel fear even though there is actually no danger. Or if you see a black and white car and you think it's a real cop car, you might get nervous and slow down. But when it passes you and its some high school kid in an old cop car stripped of all authority, you suddenly feel very different. What's in our minds affects the way we live.

Christianity is based on historical, theological, and practical truth. But even though Christianity is true, if we don't mentally accept the facts, we will not experience the blessings God is offering us.

We need to educate our minds on truth so we can experience this truth in our lives. As Martin Loyd-Jones said, "Doctrine is always to be applied, it is never to be considered as an end and of itself." We must also start with the mind because, as Warren Wiersbe said, "Satan knows if he can keep us ignorant, he can keep us impotent."

2 Corinthians 4:4 states, "The god of this age has blinded the minds of unbelievers, so that they cannot see the light of the gospel that displays the glory of Christ, who is the image of God." Satan works through our false beliefs about ourselves. He's not the father of power, he's not the father of possession, he's not the father of brute force, he's not the father of fear tactics, but he is the father of lies. He knows if he can get us to believe lies, he can get us to live a lie. Therefore, we must pay attention to our minds if we hope to live free for God:

> *"Those who are dominated by the sinful nature think about sinful things, but those who are controlled by the Holy Spirit think about things that please the Spirit. [6] So letting your sinful nature control your mind leads to death. But letting the Spirit control your mind leads to life and peace." (Romans 8:5-6)*

> *"Don't copy the behavior and customs of this world, but let God transform you into a new person by changing the way you think. Then you will learn to know God's will for you, which is good and pleasing and perfect." (Romans 12:2)*

These verses teach us that the more deeply you know and understand the truth of what Christ has already made you into, the more this is going to play out in your life. The more deeply you understand and believe the fullness of your justification, the more this is going to bear fruit in your sanctification.

As one commonly used sermon illustration explains: When a new agent for the U.S. Treasury is being trained to detect counterfeit money, how do you think they are taught to decipher between the fake bills from the real money? Do they look at counterfeit currency all day? Do they educate themselves about inks, watermarks, and paper quality? Believe it or not, they don't! Their preparation consists of one primary thing: countless training time of touching, scrutinizing, and smelling real money. Why? Because if someone wants to know the genuine from the artificial, they don't need to know every artificial example. They only need to know the truth so they can detect every fake.

That's what Paul is doing in Romans 6:3-10. He's instructing people in the truth about their position in Christ now that they are saved so they can detect when the counterfeit self is trying to take over.

Your actions are a reflection of what you believe. As Martin Loyd-Jones said, "Sanctification proceeds as we are led by the Holy Spirit to draw deductions from the doctrine of justification." Romans 6:11-14explains:

> *So you also should consider yourselves to be dead to the power of sin and alive to God through Christ Jesus. [12] Do not let sin control the way you live; do not give in to sinful desires. [13] Do not let any part of your body become an instrument of evil to serve sin. Instead, give yourselves completely to God, for you were dead, but now you have new life. So use your whole body as an instrument to do what is right for the glory of God. [14] Sin is no longer your master, for you no longer live under the requirements of the law. Instead, you live under the freedom of God's grace.*

Romans 6:11is the first time in the whole book of Romans where Paul tells his readers to actually do something. Every verse up to this point has been used to explain what is true. It's all been facts. But now that Paul has thoroughly explained what is true, he says if you want to experience this truth, you need to "consider" (ESV/NLT) or "count"

(NIV) or "reckon" (KJV) yourselves dead to sin but alive to God.

This word "count" means something more than "think" or "believe" or "know." It means "to take into account, to calculate, to estimate." It's the difference between possessing a check and cashing a check. Romans 6:11 means that not only are we supposed to believe what God says is true, we are supposed to apply this truth to the reality that we live in. It's supposed to shape the way we live in the world around us.

In Romans 6:11 we are told to apply our beliefs to our lives. Then, in Romans 6:12-13, we are told to now exercise our will power. These verses are not talking about "free will" but rather about the "freed will." Our wills used to be enslaved to sin, but now God has truly set us free when we put our faith in Christ. And the more deeply we believe that we are free, the more empowerment we receive by the Holy Spirit to live free in our lives.

Sin does not have control over the true you in Christ. However, what the sinful nature can still have control over is your body. The body itself is not sinful. But the body, mind, and emotions can be controlled either by the power of sin or by your true self in Christ. So to conclude, let's look one more time at Romans 6:11-14 (NIV):

> In the same way, count yourselves dead to sin but alive to God in Christ Jesus. [12] Therefore do not let sin reign in your mortal body so that you obey its evil desires. [13] Do not offer any part of yourself to sin as an instrument of wickedness, but rather offer yourselves to God as those who have been brought from death to life; and offer every part of yourself to him as an instrument of righteousness. [14] For sin shall no longer be your master, because you are not under the law, but under grace.

This "therefore" in Romans 6:12 is really the key to the whole chapter. Romans 6:1-11 lay the ground work of truth and Romans 6:12-14 command us to apply this truth. We have been given a freedom in Christ that actually affects our lives. It's as if Paul is saying "Believe the truth that you are a new person. Believe it so deeply you are counting on it. Christ has set you free. You are justified. You were made right with God. You are a new person with a new life. The old has gone and the new has come. The sin in your body is not the real you. You are new. *Therefore* live free."

Questions:

1. How do our beliefs affect our actions?

2. Read Romans 6:11-12. Why can a Christian now resist sin?

Reflection Questions:

1. If God's grace is endless, can we sin anytime, anyway, without repenting, and still consider ourselves a Christian?

2. How does justification affect our sanctification?

3. Jesus said, "If you hold to my teaching, you are really my disciples. Then you will know the truth, and the truth will set you free" (John 8:31-32). Knowing the truth about who you are in Christ is key for your freedom. Below are a list of Bible verses that explain God's grace and what he's done for Christians. Pick one and write it down.

(Pick one: Galatians 3:26, 1 John 3:1, Romans 5:1, Romans 6:4, Romans 6:6-7, Ephesians 2:10, Galatians 2:20, 2 Corinthians 5:15-17 Romans 8:1-4 ,Romans 8:9-11, Romans 8:15, Ephesians 4:24, Ephesians 2, Ephesians 5:8, Colossians 1:21-23, Colossians 2:9-10, Colossians 3:1-17, Psalm 103:1-5, Psalm 103:12, Psalm 37:23-24, Philippians 2:13, Philippians 3:9, 1 Corinthians 1:30, 2 Corinthians 3:5-6, 2 Corinthians 5:21, 2 Corinthians 6:18, John 8:36, 1 Peter 2:9)

4. Explain what you learned from this verse.

Getting Started: How do you feel about junk mail compared to a personal letter from someone you love and who loves you? How is the Bible different from every other book?

What Is the Word of God All About?

Life is a journey that never stops. We are always moving forward, therefore we are always making decisions on which direction we are traveling. One wrong turn here or there can really get us lost. Where you go for answers and direction in life will make all the difference. Christians will always have to make the choice: Will we seek worldly wisdom or biblical wisdom?

In the age of information and when there is academically trained professional for everything, we are pressured into listening to the "experts." With all their scientific data, sophisticated arguments, and educational titles behind their names, we can sometimes feel we must listen to the wisdom of the world before consulting the word of God. Sometimes we even seek to validate the Bible with worldly evidence rather than to interpret the evidence of the experts through God's wisdom in the Bible.

Faith in God means interpreting everything through his word, not interpreting his word through everything in the world. Worldly wisdom that contradicts God's word will always lead us to severe consequences. The Bible does not condemn all forms of modern wisdom, but it certainly warns us not to believe all forms of wisdom just because it is modern (Ephesians 4:14).

The Bible is certainly *like* a guide book, an instructional manual, or even a text book. But these analogies are not good enough. The Bible is more than a book that tells you what to do. The Bible is primarily a book about a person you need to know. The word of God is like a text book in some ways, but in more ways it like a love letter written by God directly to humans.

What is this love letter about? The Bible gives us instructions about many specific things. It teaches us how to live a godly life. It tells us what went wrong in the human story (sin) and what God did to save us for his glory (the gospel of Jesus Christ). But if you wanted to summarize the Bible in the simplest, most direct way possible, the Bible is primarily about Jesus Christ.

Certainly his name is not on every page. But in every story, every theme, every truth found in the Bible – Jesus is the key that unlocks it all for us. Without Jesus being the center of what you learn from the Bible, you are simply learning morality rather than Christianity.

When Jesus rose from the grave and was talking to two men traveling on the Emmaus Road, Luke 24:27states, "Then Jesus took them through the writings of Moses and all the prophets, explaining from all the Scriptures the things concerning himself." In John 5:39-40, Jesus proclaimed to the legalists who were seeking salvation through works, "You search the Scriptures because you think they give you eternal life. But the Scriptures point to me! Yet you refuse to come to me to receive this life."

The Old and New Testament and all the 66 books were written by over 40 different authors, on three different continents, in three different languages, and over a 1500 year span. And yet despite its variety in tone, genre, and style, its content is perfectly consistent. While at first glance this does not always seem apparent, the main message of the Bible becomes crystal clear once you realize the whole thing, OT and NT, is pointing to Jesus Christ.

Abraham taking his one and only son who is caring a stack of wood on his back going up the mountain to be sacrificed (just as God's only Son carried the cross to his sacrificial death); one man's (David) victory over the enemy (Goliath) brining freedom to all of God's chosen people even though they did nothing to deserve it (just as Christ's victory sets all Christians free); Elijah ascending but leaving his spirit to his disciple Elisha (just as the Holy Spirit came into Jesus followers once he ascended); Jonah being swallowed in the belly of a fish for three days and then raising from the fish to pronounce the truth to a rebellious nation who then repents (just as Jesus was three days in the grave and then rose); Joseph being persecuted by his brothers which in the end was God's plan to save the brothers and the Egyptians (just as the Jews crucified Jesus, but through his death he offers salvation to the Jews and Gentiles); Moses who represents the law not being the one who brings the people into the promise land but Joshua (whose name in Greek is "Jesus") is then the one who brings the people into the promise land (just as we cannot enter heaven through the law but through Jesus)– all of it is pointing to the Gospel of Jesus Christ.

The entire word of God is consistently about Jesus Christ because all of Scripture is God breathed (2 Timothy 3:16), which means it was all inspired *by* the Holy Spirit, written *through* the hands of men. Like Mary being a vessel for the body of Jesus who was conceived by the Holy Spirit, the authors of the Bible were vessels for the Holy

Spirit's message. The truth in them was conceived by the Holy Spirit but written through their hands.

The Bible makes clear that the Holy Spirit's primary action is to bear witness about Jesus Christ. When the Holy Spirit is present and manifesting, he is always lifting up the name of Jesus. It makes perfect and consistent sense, therefore, that if the Holy Spirit truly wrote the Holy Scriptures, then the Scriptures are going to be all about Jesus Christ.

No book written over such a long period of time by so many different authors using so many different genres has ever nor will ever be so consistent in its content. The Bible is clearly a divine book because it is truly a divine miracle that it is so perfectly consistent in its teaching and doctrine.

The Bible, illuminated by the Holy Spirit, is God's primary and most efficient way of communicating truth to his people. Through the Bible, we learn about what is wrong, what is right, how to be saved, how to be transformed, how to live life for God, and most importantly, how Jesus Christ is the key to everything.

Questions:

1. What is your experience with reading the Bible? Do you find it easy to read or difficult? Why?

2. How would you describe the Bible? Do you think of it more like a text book, history book, love letter, or some other example not listed here?

Why Is the Word of God Vital for Transformation?

If we don't know what the truth is, how will we know when lies come against us? If we don't have a fixed point as we travel, like the Northern Star, how will we know if we are traveling in the correct direction? As humans, we have a tendency to believe what we feel like in each moment. Our feelings change often, therefore our beliefs change often.

The Bible is so key for transformation because it teaches us what's true regardless of our current feelings or circumstances. Not only does the word of God teach us the truth, it also teaches us how to apply that truth to our lives. Psalm 119:9-16 says:

> *How can a young person stay pure? By obeying your word. [10] I have tried hard to find you— don't let me wander from your commands. [11] I have hidden your word in my heart, that I might not sin against you. [12] I praise you, O Lord; teach me your decrees. [13] I have recited aloud all the regulations you have given us. [14] I have rejoiced in your laws as much as in riches. [15] I will study your commandments and reflect on your ways. [16] I will delight in your decrees and not forget your word.*

The Bible is of no value to us if we do not actually obey what it says. James 1:22-25 states:

> *But don't just listen to God's word. You must do what it says. Otherwise, you are only fooling yourselves. [23] For if you listen to the word and don't obey, it is like glancing at your face in a mirror. [24] You see yourself, walk away, and forget what you look like. [25] But if you look carefully into the perfect law that sets you free, and if you do what it says and don't forget what you heard, then God will bless you for doing it.*

In 1 Samuel 6 the ark of the Lord is in the possession of the ungodly Philistines (the ark was where the manifest presence of God used to dwell). God sends plagues on the Philistines, so they send the ark back to Israel on a cart (1 Samuel 6:7).

Years later when David wants to bring the ark back to Jerusalem, he too uses a cart to transport it. However, this was not what God commanded. God had specific instructions that the ark was to be transported by poles (1 Chronicles 15:15). When the ark began to fall off the cart, Uzzah tried to catch it with his hand, "The LORD's anger burned against Uzzah because of his irreverent act; therefore God struck him down, and he died there beside the ark of God" (2 Samuel 6:7, NIV).

God had specific instructions in his word on how to transport the ark. These instructions were for the people's good because God knows how holy he is, so he knew that the people had to treat him a certain way or his holiness would breakout against them.

David was led astray by the worldly wisdom of the Philistines. Instead of judging what the Philistines did by comparing it to what God said in his word, David followed their example blindly, and it cost him and others dearly.

In the same way, God gives us instructions on how to live in the grace of Jesus Christ so his holiness will not breakout against us. If we hope to be blessed and live in right relationship with God, we must not anger his holiness by following the sinful practices of the world that contradict his word. All the knowledge of nonbelievers is not automatically wrong. God often uses modern wisdom (like modern medicine) for his glory. But we must interpret the wisdom of the world through God's wisdom and not the other way around. When David repented of his errors he stated:

> *"It was because you, the Levites, did not bring it up the first time that the LORD our God broke out in anger against us. We did not inquire of him about how to do it in the prescribed way." So the priests*

and Levites consecrated themselves in order to
bring up the ark of the LORD, the God of Israel.
And the Levites carried the ark of God with the
poles on their shoulders, as Moses had commanded
in accordance with the word of the LORD.
(1 Chronicles 15:13-15, NIV)

The Bible was written through God's Spirit, therefore if we want to live in the Spirit we must live by his word. We must bury God's wisdom deep in our hearts so it will be a well of life flowing out into every decision we make. David's problems arrived because his knowledge of God's truth was lacking. God knew the king of Israel would have to make countless decisions, so he instructed every king to know the word of God:

> *When he takes the throne of his kingdom, he is to*
> *write for himself on a scroll a copy of this law,*
> *taken from that of the Levitical priests. It is to be*
> *with him, and he is to read it all the days of his life*
> *so that he may learn to revere the LORD his God*
> *and follow carefully all the words of this law and*
> *these decrees. (Deuteronomy 17:18-19, NIV)*

May we too know God's word so well, reading it "all the days of [our] life so that [we] may learn to revere the Lord." We must not fall to the temptation to rely on the wisdom of modern man over the wisdom of God. The modern way is not always the wrong way, but it's not always the right way either. God's word is the only source of truth that stands the test of time and is always right. It was true from the beginning of time and it will be true forever (Matthew 24:35).

Let us not have to say again and again in life, "We did not inquire of him about how to do it in the prescribed way." When a decision must be made and the worldly wisdom contradicts the biblical wisdom, choose God's way. God loves to instruct us through his word and by his Spirit, we

just have to spend the time reading the Bible and listening
to the Spirit's instruction to us.

Questions:

1. Do the Bible and modern wisdom always contradict each other? Give some examples to prove your point.

2. Do you think God gives us passes when we don't know something that is in his word? Explain.

How Can I Learn and Live the Word of God?

The Holy Spirit certainly speaks to us personally, but whenever he speaks it always correspond and never contradicts God's written word. The Holy Spirit does not speak "new" revelations to Christians, but he does apply the Bible to our lives in new and personal ways all the time.

There are many techniques to study the Bible that we simply don't have time to talk about here. The most important thing is that you read it yourself (or listen to it if you can't read well). We need to read it every day, memorize it as much as we can, and seek its truth in all our decisions. Let's read Psalm 119:9-16 once again:

> *How can a young person stay pure? By obeying your word. [10] I have tried hard to find you— don't let me wander from your commands. [11] I have hidden your word in my heart, that I might not sin against you. [12] I praise you, O Lord; teach me your decrees. [13] I have recited aloud all the regulations you have given us. [14] I have rejoiced in your laws as much as in riches. [15] I will study your commandments and reflect on your ways. [16] I will delight in your decrees and not forget your word.*

Psalm 119:9 tells us what the most important thing is when it comes to the Bible – obey it! No amount of knowledge matters at all until we apply it to our lives. If we read the Bible daily but ignore what we read, we are wasting our time.

Psalm 119:9-11 gives us the motivation to read the Bible. If we don't follow what God has said in his word, our lives will be impure, we will sin against God, and we will be miserable because of this. All blessings are by grace, but when we receive grace it empowers us to obey the word of God which results in natural, good consequences. The more we know God's word, the greater our opportunity of knowing God more personally, which is the greatest blessing of all.

Psalm 119:12-16 is our game plan going forward. Learning the word of God is not a onetime thing. There's always more truth to know and God continues to help us see new things even in Bible verses we've read hundreds of times. Every day we must reflect on God's ways, recite them aloud, and we must not forget the truths we have learned. When we try hard to know God, he always rewards our efforts with a deeper relationship with himself.

There are endless pieces of advice on how you can learn the word of God better and better. But overall, you must be intentional. Without putting in the work, you won't learn or live the word of God. Seek the help of others, listen to good preaching, read books about how to understand the Bible, but most importantly read it for yourself as much as possible in a translation you understand.

Questions:

1. Why is consistency so important in learning the Bible?

2. Look at Psalm 119:9-16. What verse do you identify with the most? Why?

Reflection Questions:

1. Do you believe the whole Bible points to Jesus? Why or why not?

2. What benefits are there to memorizing Bible verses?

3. Many people find the morning the best time to read the Bible because it helps prepare them for the day ahead. What is your plan for having a devotional time in your life?

4. What hurdles or questions are still keeping you from reading or listening to the Bible? How can you overcome these hurdles?

Week 7
The Importance of Prayer
Key Text: Luke 18:1-8

Getting Started: When you think of "prayer," what comes to your mind?

What Is Christian Prayer?

Prayer is crucial for the health of a Christian's heart. But what is prayer? Prayer is not unique to Christianity. Almost all religions have some form of prayer rituals and practices. But when we as Christians pray, we are coming into the presence of God through the gospel of Jesus Christ.

Prayer is more than making requests of God. Prayer is ultimately being in conversation with God through listening and speaking.

There are many types of prayer: praise/thanksgiving, confession, intercession (prayers for others), supplication (prayers requests for self), and meditation/listening. But prayer can be more than all of these things. Essentially, prayer is actively walking with God in a personal, moment to moment relationship.

When we begin to understand the full scope of what prayer can be with God, suddenly Luke 18:1 begins to make a lot more sense, *"One day Jesus told his disciples a story to show that they should always pray and never give up."*

A rich, deep, profound, moment by moment relationship with the Father, Son, and Holy Spirit is exactly what our hearts need to stay alive. Prayer and never giving up are tied together for the Christian. If we neglect God in prayer, our hearts will be hungry, lonely, directionless, and we will turn from God in sin.

We were made to listen to him and to talk to him; but because of sin everything got messed up (Genesis 1-3). Ultimately we lose heart not because the world is hard to live in; we lose heart because we try to live in the world without God, which is more than hard . . . it's impossible.

Luke 18:1 tells us that the reason Jesus shares this parable is so we will be able to pray more and not give up in our Christian walk. But how is this parable going to help us do those two things?

Jesus tells us a story that teaches us about God because the deeper our understanding of God, the more passionate and powerful our prayers will become. In Martin Loyd-Jone's book called *Revival*, he states, "Great prayer is always the outcome of great understanding. . . . It is when a man is in the furnace of affliction, it is then, indeed, that he falls back upon certain fundamental truths of which he is absolutely sure and certain. The key to great praying is a deep knowledge and grasp of the doctrine of grace."

Parables, like the one told in Luke 18:1-8, always compare or contrast something (or someone) in Jesus' story with something (or someone) in real life. In the case of the unjust judge, Jesus is simply contrasting this judge with God. Everything we will learn about this judge will take us into a deeper understanding of God by seeing how totally different God is compared to the unjust judge. And the more we know God, the more our prayer life will benefit.

Questions:

1. How would you define "prayer?"

2. What is Jesus' purpose in telling this parable about a poor widow and an unjust judge? (Note: The answer is found in Luke 18:1.)

Why Is Prayer Key for Transformation?

There was a judge in a certain city," Jesus said, "who neither feared God nor cared about people. ³ A widow of that city came to him repeatedly, saying, 'Give me justice in this dispute with my enemy.'" (Luke 18:2-3)

Luke 18:1 makes it known that Jesus wants us to always be in communion with God. He then instantly motivates us in Luke 18:2 to passionately pursue this relationship by giving us a picture of God's absolute goodness, holiness, and love.

The first thing we learn about this judge is that he "neither feared God nor cared about people." But remember, the whole point of Jesus' parable is to show us how God is totally different than this unjust judge. Jesus points out the bad and corrupt character of the judge to highlight the totally good and pure character of God. By stating the unjust judge doesn't care about the widow, Jesus is teaching us that God really does care about us. 1 Peter 5:7 states, "Give all your worries and cares to God, for he cares about you."

In Dr. Dobson's book called *Brining Up Boys*, he instructs that during the teen years, kids will find it much harder to listen to the advice of their parents if they felt unloved in childhood. He instructs parents, "The best way to avoid this teenage time bomb is to diffuse it in childhood . . . Begin now to build a relationship that will see you through the storms of adolescence." Dr. Leman, in *Parenting Your Powerful Child*, also states, "They don't care what you know . . . until they know that you care."

Why does this relate to prayer? Just like a child who rebels against her parents because she doubts their love for her, if we don't believe deep in our being that God really cares for us, we will find it very hard to "always pray" and thus we will lose heart and give up (Luke 18:1).

Luke 18:3 shows us why prayer is so key for our transformation. You see, a widow in the time period of this parable would have been totally helpless in this male dominated society. History shows that widows were not even allowed to be in the courtroom unless there was absolutely no male who could plead her case.

So for this widow to be coming to the judge herself in Jesus' parable, it meant not only did she have no husband, it meant she had no son, no brother, no uncle, no nephew, no distant male cousin . . . she literally had no one to plead her case on her behalf. She was the most needy type of person in all of society. She had no hope to gain justice against her enemy except for this judge. If the judge did not act on her behalf, she was completely helpless.

Jesus is trying to point out that in reality, we are this widow. Without God showing his kindness, we would have nothing. We have enemies in the flesh, the world, and the devil, and without the power of God working through prayer, we are helpless. We are as powerless spiritually as this widow was physically.

All this is a perfect picture of the gospel. Romans 3:23 states that all have sinned and fallen short of the glory of God. Romans 8:8 states, "Those who are in the flesh cannot please God." We are all as totally helpless and in need of a redeemer as this widow. We cannot create our own transformation. Just as this widow will remain unjustified without someone helping her, we too would be unjustified without God moving on our behalf through the work of Christ (Romans 8:30).

The clear, simple, and true message of the Bible is that everything good we have is from God, not ourselves: Acts 17:25 (NIV), "And [God] is not served by human hands, as if he needed anything. Rather, he himself gives everyone life and breath and everything else." James 1:16-17 (NIV), "Don't be deceived, my dear brothers and sisters. Every good and perfect gift is from above, coming down from the

Father." The widow understood that her hope was in the hands of the judge, just as we must understand our hope is truly in the hands of God alone.

Notice what the widow did not do. She did not seek justice in her own power. She didn't turn to others once the judge refused her. Why? Because she understood that only the judge had the rightful authority to do anything about her problem. She wasn't going to take her eyes off the judge because she knew he was the only one who could truly help.

Likewise, when we begin to understand the great power of God and begin to truly believe he alone is powerful enough to help us change and transform, only then will we cry out to him day and night.

The widow is our example, for she was humble enough to know her helplessness. She went to the judge constantly because she knew she was powerless. We too should go to God constantly because we too must realize that without Christ, we really are helpless (John 15:5). A lack of consistent prayer to God is the surest sign of pride in one's self and doubt in God's power.

Questions:

1. Have you ever been in such a bad situation that you literally could not help yourself? Perhaps you needed medical attention you could not offer yourself, legal assistance you couldn't perform on your own, or housing assistance you could not afford. In situations like these, what is your attitude towards those you need?

2. Since we are spiritually helpless without God, how should we respond to him?

How Can I Pray Often and With Power?

> *One day Jesus told his disciples a story to show that they should always pray and never give up. ² "There was a judge in a certain city," he said, "who neither feared God nor cared about people. ³ A widow of that city came to him repeatedly, saying, 'Give me justice in this dispute with my enemy.' ⁴ The judge ignored her for a while, but finally he said to himself, 'I don't fear God or care about people, ⁵ but this woman is driving me crazy. I'm going to see that she gets justice, because she is wearing me out with her constant requests!'"*
>
> *Then the Lord said, "Learn a lesson from this unjust judge. ⁷ Even he rendered a just decision in the end. So don't you think God will surely give justice to his chosen people who cry out to him day and night? Will he keep putting them off? ⁸ I tell you, he will grant justice to them quickly! But when the Son of Man returns, how many will he find on the earth who have faith?" (Luke 18:1-8)*

As we have been saying throughout this chapter, the more we truly know God, the more motivation we will have to pray. Jesus is teaching us about God in this parable by contrasting him with the unjust judge. Let's gather more details about God which will help us to pray more and not give up:

Verse 2: God really cares about us, thus he wants us to talk to him and listen to him in prayer.

Verse 3-5: God doesn't answer our prayers so we will stop coming to him. God answers our prayers so we will come to him more often. Notice the unjust judge never talks to the widow; he only "said to himself." God talks to us and listens to us.

Verse 6-7: God is "sovereign" which means he is all powerful and has planned everything for his people. Notice we are a "chosen people." We should pray day and night because God is all powerful.

Verse 8: Prayer is an expression of faith in God. You can always know how much or little you believe in God by what your prayer life looks like. Limited time in prayer shows you doubt God's presence and involvement. Small requests of God show you doubt his power. When we have faith in God, we will pray often and boldly.

In closing, there are many more things we could say about prayer. Prayer is one of those topics that we as Christians should always be learning about and practicing. You will never outgrow prayer. But how should we pray? There are at least five different basic types of prayer that God wants us to do daily:

- Thanksgiving and praise: God desires our worship. In prayer we can show him the gratitude he deserves for all the good he does for us and we can praise him for his amazing character and love.

- Confession: God desires us to regularly confess our sins to him. Confession is admitting what you did wrong and asking God to forgive you through the blood of Jesus. Repentance is when we turn away from our sin and turn back to God. Confession is always the first step in repentance.

- Requests: God wants us to come to him for our every need. Asking God for things should not be the only things we pray. But this is a huge part of a healthy prayer life. God only gives us what is good for us, so he won't answer every prayer the way we asked, but he always hears us and he always does what is best for us.

- Intercession: Not only should we pray for ourselves, but we should also pray for other people. God really does bless other people through the prayers of his people. Praying for others also softens your heart towards people who have hurt you or that you want to love better.

- Listening and meditating: Prayer is a conversation and true conversation involves speaking and listening. God speaks and listens to us and he desires the same. We should regularly quiet our hearts and minds to listen to the Holy Spirit's leading in our personal lives. We should also pray the Scriptures and sit before God as we meditate over specific Bible verses. Those who consistently still their hearts to hear God are the ones who experience God's personal leading in their lives.

Just like reading your Bible, prayer is something we should do daily. It has the power to change our lives and help us grow closer to God. If you don't want to give up and lose heart in life, then as Jesus taught us in Luke 18:1-8, we must pray to God often.

Questions:

1. How do the word of God and prayer complement each other? (In other words, how does knowing the truth help you pray?)

2. Out of the five types of prayer mentioned in this chapter, what comes natural to you and what is a type of prayer you need to practice more often?

Reflection Questions:

1. What hinders you from praying to God more often? What can be done to overcome this obstacle in your prayer life?

2. How is the widow in Luke 18 an example of us all? How do you personally relate to her?

3. In what ways is God different than the unjust judge?

4. What's one new thing you learned through this chapter? What is one question you still have about prayer?

Week 8
The Importance of The Local Church
Key Text: Romans 12:1-18

Getting Started: What has been your experience with church?

What Is The Church?

Life is a journey not meant to be traveled alone. Before time even existed, God has lived within the community of the Trinity: Father, Son, and Holy Spirit. God did not need to create humans, but he chose to make us because of his love and desire to share his life with others. Therefore, since we are made in God's image, it should be no surprise to learn that humans were made to have meaningful relationships not only with God but also with other humans.

When God created Adam, the two of them had a perfect relationship with each other that was unblemished by sin. But even then God knew Adam needed another human to share life with, "Then the LORD God said, 'It is not good that the man should be alone; I will make him a helper fit for him'" (Genesis 2:28). God not only created Adam and Eve, he also gave them the ability to reproduce and populate the earth with more humans.

It was God's intention for people to love and live with other people in healthy communities. Sin, however, ruined all this. Cain and Able, sons of Adam and Eve, are examples of what has continued to happen in human relationships because of the sin within the human heart. Cain grew jealous of Able, there was conflict between them, and eventually Cain killed Able (Genesis 4).

Since sin has been introduced into human relationships, there has been a lot of problems between people, races, and countries. Conflict is the norm now. This is why God has created a new, chosen people who are unified through Jesus Christ (Galatians 3:26-29).

The gospel certainly affects individuals. To become a Christian is a personal decision between you and God. While transformation and our relationship with God must be personal, Christianity must not be private. As soon as you are converted, God transfers you into his family full of his other sons and daughters. God calls his family the church.

The church is described in many ways throughout the Bible. It is called the Bride, the family of God, Jesus' flock of sheep, God's holy nation, a kingdom of priests, and the body of Christ. The "body of Christ" is an especially helpful metaphor because it highlights the importance of each church member and what they individually contribute to the whole. Everyone is different. Everyone has different skills. And this is good. God uses this diversity to advance his kingdom for his glory:

> *Just as our bodies have many parts and each part has a special function, [5] so it is with Christ's body. We are many parts of one body, and we all belong to each other.*
>
> *[6] In his grace, God has given us different gifts for doing certain things well. So if God has given you the ability to prophesy, speak out with as much faith as God has given you. [7] If your gift is serving others, serve them well. If you are a teacher, teach well. [8] If your gift is to encourage others, be encouraging. If it is giving, give generously. If God has given you*

leadership ability, take the responsibility seriously. And if you have a gift for showing kindness to others, do it gladly. (Romans 12:4-8)

As a Christian, God has called you to live within a community of other believers. They are supposed to help you through life as you seek to live for God's glory, and you are supposed to help them as they seek to do the same. Every Christian does not have a choice to be a part of God's Universal Church. If you are a Christian, you are a part of his body, the church. However, the Universal Church is expressed in a local context. This is where each Christian must actively pursue participation within a local church.

Being a part of a local church is not an option for a Christian since it is a command by God. God has commanded each Christian to be a part of a specific church, not just the Universal Church (Hebrews 10:25, Colossians 3:16, John 17:20-21). God's commands are always for our good. God commands us to be a part of local church because he knows how impossible it will be for us to live life without the support of pastors, other believers, and a community of diverse Christians.

There are many qualities to look for in a good church. However, if you were to look for the most basic markers of a biblical church, there are two specific things to look for: 1. A true church will meet regularly to preach the word of God to a group of believers. 2. A true church will regularly perform the two biblical sacraments of communion and baptism. Mark Dever explains:

> "How do you know if what calls itself a church is indeed a church? Christians in the past thought about this. They developed the idea of "the marks of the church," that is, the characteristics that distinguish truly Christian churches. The Protestant Reformers concluded that there are two of these: the

right preaching of God's Word and the right administration of baptism and the Lord's Supper."

There are many other things a healthy church must do to effectively lead and love its members. Churches vary widely on how they operate practically and in ministry. But to be a biblical Christian church, they must at least do these two things.

<u>Questions:</u>

1. List some benefits of having other Christians to help you through life. Also list benefits of being helpful to others.

2. List some challenges of being a part of a church. What fears, hesitations, or doubts come into your mind when you think about being a part of a local church?

Why Is the Church So Important for Your Personal Transformation?

If you've ever played sports or competed in any type of competition, you know that the "home field advantage" is a big help. For example: In the NBA Finals when two teams are playing in a decisive winner-take-all game seven, the home team is 15-4. When comparing a country's medal counts between the Olympics before hosting compared to the year they did host the Olympics, the host country's medal count increased on average by twenty, with gold medal wins increasing on average by ten.

The same is true in life. God designed us to need other people and to be needed by other people. Both helping other Christians and being helped by other Christians are crucial for a healthy walk with God. We all know we function better when we have people supporting us, rooting for us, and helping us when we get bogged down.

Proverbs 13:20 says, "Walk with the wise and become wise; associate with fools and get in trouble." 1 Corinthians 15:33 (NIV) explains, "Do not be misled: Bad company corrupts good character." As one popular phrase puts it, "Show me your friends and I will show you your future."

Walking through life with other Christians is key for transformation. As we have discussed throughout this study, justification happens in a moment, but sanctification takes a lifetime. There will be many ups and downs on this journey of sanctification. To live a full life for God, you need people to celebrate the highs with you and support you through the lows.

Additionally, to live a full life, you must also be there for other people. As Paul said in Acts 20:35, "And I have been a constant example of how you can help those in need by working hard. You should remember the words of the Lord Jesus: 'It is more blessed to give than to receive.'"

When we sin, other Christians should be there to help us through it and you should be there for others in their times of need as well. James 5:16, 19-20 states:

> *"Confess your sins to each other and pray for each other so that you may be healed. The earnest prayer of a righteous person has great power and produces wonderful results.*
>
> *. . . My dear brothers and sisters, if someone among you wanders away from the truth and is brought back, [20] you can be sure that whoever brings the sinner back from wandering will save that person from death and bring about the forgiveness of many sins.*

Without the support of others and being a support to others, the lure of sin is that much more tempting to us. 2 Timothy 2:22 also gives us great advice:

> *Run from anything that stimulates youthful lusts. Instead, pursue righteous living, faithfulness, love, and peace. Enjoy the companionship of those who call on the Lord with pure hearts."*

As we can see, the health of our relationships with other people who are also pursuing the Lord directly affects our own walk with God. We need other people, and other people need us.

Lastly, a local church is so important for your personal growth because we must remember what we are seeking to grow towards. The aim of our lives as Christians is now to glorify God. To glorify God we must reflect him. And to reflect God, we must live in a community of other believers because God is a relational God. In John 17:20-21, Jesus prayed on our behalf to the Father:

> *I am praying not only for these disciples but also for all who will ever believe in me through their message. [21] I pray that they will all be one, just as*

you and I are one—as you are in me, Father, and I am in you. And may they be in us so that the world will believe you sent me."

To be transformed means to bear the image of God. And to bear the image of God, we must show unity with other believers. When we show unity as Christians, this helps the world around us see God. When others see God reflected in our lives, God is glorified and others are benefited. Therefore, being a part of local church is vital for our mission to glorify God and to be transformed into his image.

1. Why is being a part of a local church so important?

2. How does showing unity with other Christians help us glorify God? How does being a part of a local church help us reach non-believers with the gospel?

How to Love and Be Loved By a Local Church?

The phrase "church membership" is not found in the Bible; however, it is a principle found in Scripture. Much like other theological words like "Trinity" that are not found in Scripture but describe a truth seen in the Bible, "church membership" is a truth seen in a variety of passages. For example, Hebrews 13:7, 17 says:

> *Remember your leaders who taught you the word of God. Think of all the good that has come from their lives, and follow the example of their faith. . . . [17] Obey your spiritual leaders, and do what they say. Their work is to watch over your souls, and they are accountable to God. Give them reason to do this with joy and not with sorrow. That would certainly not be for your benefit.*

Notice the words "your leaders." This means there are leaders in one church that are different leaders from another church. God expects us to be committed to a specific local church with specific pastors and church members. As a member of a local church, you have obligations to "your" leaders and other church members in a different way than you do towards the pastors and church members from the local church down the street.

So the first way to be a part of local church is to commit to a specific group of Christians and leaders. You don't have to use the words "church membership" and your local church may change sometimes for varying reasons. But in general, you should have a specific church who is committed to your well-being and you are committed to their well-being.

Being a part of a local church is a relationship. To have successful relationships, there must be mutual respect, give-and-take, and common bonds that keep you together. All the principles that apply to having a healthy relationship with a person apply to having a healthy relationship with your church. One of the best places for advice on having a healthy relationship with other Christians and a local church is found in Romans 12:1-18. It reads:

> *And so, dear brothers and sisters, I plead with you to give your bodies to God because of all he has done for you. Let them be a living and holy sacrifice—the kind he will find acceptable. This is truly the way to worship him. ² Don't copy the behavior and customs of this world, but let God transform you into a new person by changing the way you think. Then you will learn to know God's will for you, which is good and pleasing and perfect.*
>
> *³Because of the privilege and authority God has given me, I give each of you this warning: Don't think you are better than you really are. Be honest in your evaluation of yourselves, measuring yourselves by the faith God has given us. ⁴ Just as our bodies have many parts and each part has a special function, ⁵ so it is with Christ's body. We are many parts of one body, and we all belong to each other.*
>
> *⁶ In his grace, God has given us different gifts for doing certain things well. So if God has given you the ability to prophesy, speak out with as much faith as God has given you. ⁷ If your gift is serving others, serve them well. If you are a teacher, teach well. ⁸ If your gift is to encourage others, be encouraging. If it is giving, give generously. If God has given you leadership ability, take the responsibility seriously. And if you have a gift for showing kindness to others, do it gladly.*
>
> *⁹ Don't just pretend to love others. Really love them. Hate what is wrong. Hold tightly to what is good. ¹⁰ Love each other with genuine affection, and take delight in honoring each other. ¹¹ Never be*

*lazy, but work hard and serve the Lord
enthusiastically. ¹² Rejoice in our confident hope. Be
patient in trouble, and keep on praying. ¹³ When
God's people are in need, be ready to help them.
Always be eager to practice hospitality.*

*¹⁴ Bless those who persecute you. Don't curse them;
pray that God will bless them. ¹⁵ Be happy with
those who are happy, and weep with those who
weep. ¹⁶ Live in harmony with each other. Don't be
too proud to enjoy the company of ordinary people.
And don't think you know it all!*

*¹⁷ Never pay back evil with more evil. Do things in
such a way that everyone can see you are
honorable. ¹⁸ Do all that you can to live in peace
with everyone.*

Romans 12:1-2 starts with personal transformation. To love
others well and to be in healthy relationships, it all starts
with our personal relationship with God through Jesus
Christ. We must be filled with God's love before we have
any love to give. This transformation process is something
every Christian should be doing together, "And so, dear
brothers and sisters. . ." (Romans 12:1).

Romans 12:3 talks about the need for humility and not
comparing yourself to others. We must not think too highly
of ourselves if we want to have good relationships with
others.

Romans 12:4-8 highlights the need for mutual respect and
using our gifts to serve others. God has blessed us with
unique talents and gifts not to exalt ourselves but to love
other people. Offering your service to other Christians is
very important if you want to be a part of a healthy local
church.

Romans 12:9-13 explains the importance of love in the
local church. We all know when love is not genuine. We
can't control what others do, but we can seek to offer

genuine love to others through the power God gives us through his Spirit. Be ready to help others. If you go to church with an attitude of service and generosity, you will always get more in return than you give out.

Romans 12:14-18 is all about dealing with conflict. To have a long and healthy relationship with anyone, including with a local church, we must learn to be peacemakers when conflict arises. No matter how good your church is, no matter how stable its foundation, and no matter how well intentioned the people involved, conflict always happens. We must be prepared to meet conflict head-on with love, biblical wisdom, and a heart seeking reconciliation whenever possible.

In summary, being a part of a local church will be one of the hardest things you do but also one of the best. If we want to live the Christian life well and be transformed for the glory of God, being a part of a local church is vitally important.

Questions:

1. What are some principles you have learned that help create healthy relationships?

2. Read Romans 12:1-18. What verse sticks out to you and why?

Reflection Questions:

1. If you are not currently a part of a local church, how might your past experiences with church be affecting your willingness to join a church now? What can you do about this so you are ready and willing to join a local church?

2. A church is not a building. In your own words, how would you describe what the church really is according to the Bible?

3. Do you think the support of other people is important for your growth as a Christian? Why or why not?

4. What are ways you would like to serve in a local church? What are ways other people from a local church could serve you?

ApplyGodsWord.com

For blogs, videos, free eBooks, and for more resources by Mark Ballenger, visit ApplyGodsWord.com.

You can also connect with Mark in these ways as well:

Twitter

Facebook

YouTube

(Just go to these social media platforms and search "ApplyGodsWord.com" and you should see the AGW pages/channels.)

Email: MarkBallenger@ApplyGodsWord.com

Lastly, if you enjoyed this study, would you consider writing a short review on the Amazon product page? The more reviews a book gets the more Amazon will promote it to other people. Let's spread the word of God together. Thanks for considering this!

Printed in Great Britain
by Amazon

16638260R00072